I CAN READ ABOUT

CHRISTOPHER COLUMBUS

Written by David Knight

Illustrated by Herb Mott

Troll Associates

Christopher Columbus was born in 1451 in Genoa, Italy. When he was a young boy, he helped in his father's wool weaving shop. Every day, he watched the ships sail in and out of the busy seaport. And he dreamed of being a sailor.

He loved to listen to the stories the sailors told.
He heard stories about other ports they visited.
There were tales about sea monsters in
the Sea of Darkness. There were stories
about strange, faraway lands.
Christopher dreamed of the day
when he would be old enough
to go to sea.

By the time he was 20, young Christopher's dream had come true. He no longer worked at his father's looms. Now he was a sailor.

On one voyage, his ship was attacked by pirates.
Columbus was injured. When his ship began to sink,
he jumped into the sea. He grabbed a floating
piece of wood, and was able to reach shore.

When Columbus was 25 years old,
he went to Lisbon, Portugal. Lisbon was
a busy seaport. His brother, Bartholomew,
owned a shop in Lisbon. In the shop
were many maps and charts.

Columbus had read about a place called Cathay, or China, which was part of the "Indies." The Indies lay far to the east, and they were rich with spices and jewels. There were even palaces made of gold. Marco Polo had reached China by land. Now a sea route to the Indies was needed.

Portuguese sailors were trying to reach the Indies by sailing around Africa. But Columbus began to think about reaching the Indies by sailing west — across the Sea of Darkness — across the Atlantic Ocean.

As the years passed, Columbus became a ship's captain. He married the daughter of a Portuguese sea captain, and they had a son. Unfortunately, Columbus' wife
died soon afterward.

Columbus had not given up his dream of reaching the Indies by sailing west. He asked the King of Portugal to give him ships for a voyage to the Indies. The king refused. Then Columbus sent his brother, Bartholomew, to ask the King of England and the King of France for help. Perhaps they would supply the ships.

Columbus moved to Spain. He put his young son in a school for boys. The school was run by friars. One of the friars listened to Columbus' dream of sailing west to reach the Indies. He wrote to Queen Isabella of Spain.

Before long, Columbus was telling Queen Isabella and King Ferdinand about his dream. They listened closely. The queen was interested, but Spain was at war, and a voyage would be expensive. Columbus would have to wait.

Columbus waited and waited.

When the war was over, Queen Isabella sent for Columbus. She wanted gold and riches from the Indies. So she gave Columbus what he asked for. He could have three ships for the voyage. He could be governor of any lands he discovered. He could share in all the riches, and he could have the title, "Admiral of the Ocean Sea."

Columbus tried to find sailors for his
ships — the *Niña,* the *Pinta,* and the *Santa Maria.*
It was not easy. Not many men wanted to cross
the Sea of Darkness. Finally, sixty sailors
were gathered together.

The ships were loaded with food
and fresh water for the long voyage.
They were stocked with things to trade
for the riches of the Indies.
At last, the small wooden ships hoisted
their sails.

They sailed out of the port of Palos, Spain,
on August 3, 1492.

Only three days later,
the *Pinta's* rudder broke. It
was repaired at the Canary Islands,
off the coast of Africa.

Then the ships set sail again. Before long, they left the Canary Islands far behind. The "Admiral of the Ocean Sea" looked at his compass. He was heading west—into the Sea of Darkness.

They sailed and sailed. Days became weeks.
Week after week passed. Still, there was no sign of
land. The sailors grew restless. The water supply
was running low. The men wanted to turn back.

Columbus tried to cheer them up.
But each day was the same. There was no land.
The men complained and grumbled. They even
began to carry knives. Would they mutiny?
Would they take over the ship and
return to Spain?

No one had ever sailed
so far into the Sea of Darkness.
The men did not want to go any farther.
Finally Columbus said, "We will sail for
three more days. Then, if we do not see land,
we will turn back."

Two days later, they saw some birds, and then a floating branch with leaves. Columbus knew they must be nearing land. Everyone watched the horizon. Where was the land? Each sailor wanted to be the first to see it.

That night, Columbus thought he saw a light in the distance. He looked again, but it was gone. Then it reappeared. Soon everybody saw the light.

All night, the three ships
kept sailing toward it.

When the sun rose on October 12, Columbus saw a beautiful sight. Before him were sandy beaches and palm trees. He named the island "San Salvador."

Before noon, the sailors were walking up the beach. They were glad to be off the ships at last. Seventy-one days at sea was a long time.

The people on the island were friendly. Columbus called them "Indians," because he thought he had reached an island in the Indies. Actually, he had landed on one of the Bahama Islands, a few hundred miles southeast of Florida.

Columbus and his men traded with
the Indians. But there were no spices, and
no jewels. And there were no golden palaces.
So after a few days, the three ships set sail
again. Soon they discovered Cuba, and then
Haiti, which Columbus named "Hispaniola."

On Christmas Eve, along the coast of Hispaniola,
the *Santa Maria* struck a coral reef. The ship
was so badly damaged that it could not be fixed.

Columbus decided to leave some of the sailors on Hispaniola. Wood from the wreck of the *Santa Maria* was used to build a fort. Then Columbus decided to return to Spain.

The voyage back across the Sea of Darkness was not easy. Strong winds and huge waves separated the *Niña* and the *Pinta*. Columbus wondered if he would ever reach home. So he wrote a note, and put it in a barrel. Then he threw the barrel in the sea. If the *Niña* did not reach home, perhaps the barrel would.

The barrel did not reach Spain. But the *Niña* did. On March 15, it arrived in the port of Palos, Spain. The *Pinta* arrived soon afterward.

King Ferdinand and Queen Isabella named Columbus "Viceroy," or governor of the Indies. They asked him to make another voyage. They wanted him to reach the mainland of the Indies and look for gold.

Between 1493 and 1504, Columbus made three more voyages to
the New World. He continued to search for the great cities
Marco Polo had written about, but he never found them. When
he returned to Hispaniola, he learned that all his men
had died. The Indians, whom the men had treated badly, had killed them.

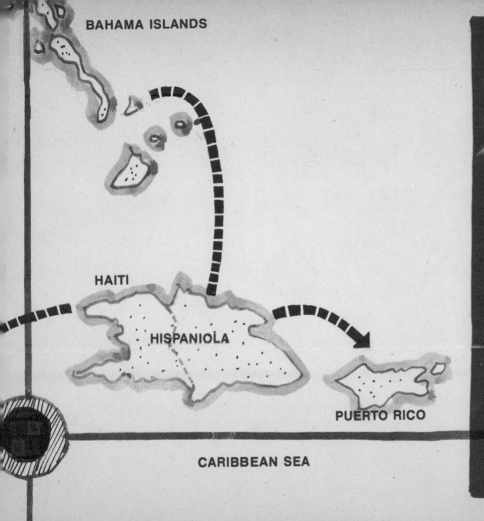

BAHAMA ISLANDS

HAITI

HISPANIOLA

PUERTO RICO

CARIBBEAN SEA

Columbus discovered more islands, including Jamaica and Puerto Rico. He also reached the continent of South America, which he called the "Other World." He was convinced that the mainland of China and the riches of the Indies were nearby.

On his last voyage, Columbus learned that still another ocean lay on the other side of Panama.

But Queen Isabella died before Columbus could tell her about it. The king's feelings toward Columbus had changed, and the king refused to see him.

During his final years, Columbus was disappointed and ill. His discoveries had not made him rich. And he was no longer governor of the lands he had discovered.

Columbus died on May 20, 1506.
He never knew how important his discoveries
really were.

Christopher Columbus had spent his life trying to reach the Indies by sailing west. But instead of the Indies, he had discovered the Americas. And his voyages opened up a great new world.